S0-CTJ-719

POPE PIUS XII LIBRARY, ST. JOSEPH COL.

3 2528 07525 6836

Guards of the Heart

Guards of the Heart

Four Plays by
Joe Ross

A Blue Corner Drama
Corner Books
Los Angeles

Copyright © Joe Ross, 1990
Cover photograph: Collage by Douglas Messerli
Design: Katie Messborn
Portions of these plays have previously been published in *Aerial*;
Best American Poetry: 1988 [edited by John Ashbery]; and
Washington Review.

All rights reserved
No part of this publication may be reproduced or transmitted in any form
or by any means, electronic or mechanical, including photocopy,
recording, or any information storage or retrieval system now known or to
be invented, without permission in writing from the publisher and/or the
author and his representatives, except by a reviewer who wishes to quote
brief passages in connection with a review written for inclusion in a
magazine, newspaper or broadcast.
For professional, amateur, and stock production rights contact Corner
Books, 6148 Wilshire Boulevard, Los Angeles, California 90048, (213)
857-1115; FAX (213) 857-0143.

Library of Congress Cataloging-in-Publication Data

Ross, Joe (1960)
   Guards of the Heart: Four Plays by Joe Ross

A Blue Corner Drama   CIP   91-050127
ISBN: 1-55713-082-5

FIRST EDITION
10 9 8 7 6 5 4 3 2 1

A Blue Corner Drama
6148 Wilshire Boulevard
Los Angeles, California 90048

for Deb & Doug

Contents

A CHOICE OF HISTORY

to those who can see what is can be

ACT I

[Setting: Black blue ivory or green
as it screams rhythms night
rolling through hills and seeking beauty
after days daze near the end of word
a dialogue turns and frees its mind]

SCENE I *[The Introduction]*

HISS: Come on now,
we hear spirits in spite—
attempts sometimes follow.
See the pause.
There are gaps or fears or internal pangs.
Sliced action is all one needs to move.
Here—is there,
yesterday, today and tomorrow
a sequence in a point plotted no where.
I call back with the answers, right now.
The old or the remembered
not the same, in mind or
out of state, a wood is a board
or trees grove
to a tern for a nest, home.
Is there too many? Okay
I'll take one back.
Footprints before a walk

causes no causes.

TORY: I used to care about time but they stole the clocks.

HISS: Water gives life,

or takes the attention anyway.

Shift, and

hello frozen tundra;

Isn't it cold, here

have my parka,

the jungle is disappearing.

TORY: Lines yell to edges,

but we were taught old school.

If I were young enough or free

I could invent a friend

but they robbed all of us with, ''This is Truth.''

HISS: Come back down here, your seat is getting cold.

I was iron but now the cast is for you.

SCENE II *[Beginning Action]*

HISS: In '64 the water was ear deep in nail.

Pailing like quick sand on marble

stuck. Round or after

takes thoughts a second

or jump

and a step is finished

and repeated.

Between leaps allow the water to float on green.

Standard of the correct method

where road is forked.
With all the connections
where will we find crows,
in time?
Is next to sheep or lamb?
Walls keep the rocks from rising
to sing of liberation.

TORY: The convention was convened at start and
will continue until a speaker stops a hear.

HISS: We make the laws
and enforce by not seeing.
A rat turns to leaves
and gets caught with the better.
But stick, bounces
if you will
to a branch.
The main is never thought of.

TORY: I opened a new one and saw backwards from a front.

HISS: Turn now to either
or fall to one
a choice,
allows a retake—
it all happens now.

SCENE III *[The Confrontations Begin]*

HISS: The banging of the pipes calls riddle to mind.
See how the bronze

and silver slide in
to melt a steal
is not difficult, just flow.

TORY: I watered the measure, but bounced off
the course to the old
where everything is
solid.

HISS: Yes, the hard is heavy
to an unfaithful mind,
the spring
where a bloom was a bud,
who gives a clue
plays with mud.

TORY: I see some signs
but await a paint.
To stencil in a new design
like poundage
where shiny steel might be
a new ton away.

HISS: Give light to a dark or subtract the weight.
Shoulders can bare,
in the sun all rays
reflect a deeper need to geometry.
A tanned gent dives
with a perfect arch
to the day before.

TORY: How can I swim
with feet in concrete
with blind causes

and a doctrine of apples?
HISS: Simply peel a core of gangster's connections.
    All mobs make their own rules,
    to trap,
    an essence is
    a key to cement.

SCENE IV *[A Showdown on the Edge of Line]*

HISS: I've brought you out of line,
    where a mind takes hold.
    Any point is a loci of time's focus.
    Here, a now makes cheeses with false mice.
TORY: I smell a trap.
    But temptation was always told
    to avoid a sin
    where the hidden can upset
    a balance, to scale.
HISS: Yes, old weighings were always the standard.
    But as heavy grows
    meaningless a measure
    marks the end
    or time's illusion of solid.
TORY: For a life a real can bait a line.
    To fish a stream runs many parallels,
    but one pond is all that can be pooled.
HISS: That is the mis-take from your cue.
    Stick to one break and you'll never see,

the shark that controls your table,
play many pools to learn the game.

SCENE V *[The Conversion—Seeing a Naked Cast with Word]*

TORY: Now that I have heard your word,
　　my alliance alights my old ally and
　　I feel fly to a wing of a new freedom
　　where a conservative is a block.
HISS: I had to stone you with a rock.
　　But I grant that it's not impossible
　　to dissolve back to original flow
　　before when
　　the cast was not set.
TORY: A play is truly without an act.
　　To be caught with the curtain up
　　and the blinds down
　　leaves a green audience
　　ready for trees.
HISS: That is the root to take, to find.
　　Soil your word with a grain of seed
　　where the plant of past isn't a future.
　　Harvest.

SEEING A LAND

ACT I

[Prologue: To reach beyond a given past
remains an obstacle...blocked by what
we are trapped...words, worlds of our own making
the curtain rises, maybe...possibilities over-looked
or simply forgotten...hear characters struggle.]

SCENE I *[Gentle Trepidation]*

CAPTAIN: Wake the child who swims gold.
    The owners make feudal attempts with surfs.
    Refuse to claim a line given by a weed—
    it's sometimes healthy to eat a yelp.
MATE: Maybe so to one who fishes
    for harvest—a moon
    hangs to sun a night—
    with sword.
CAPTAIN: Yes, any free dance wields the word
    to slice a double edges on absurd.
    For you a maiden's fate awaits the call.
MATE: White is ready
    but day blinds the glow.
    It's the reflection which swells for all to see.
CAPTAIN: So you doubt the gentleness of a buff.
    For new it places a zone with mist.
    Hear the beckon that the fog horns.
MATE: There's a dive

where a rock waits to break,
or breach—
a surface promise.
I can't yet lend faith my shovel.
CAPTAIN: Alright slow your worms with hedge.
There's still children for rose and ring.
Any tree is given a chance to leave,
or riding with a sail
rocks a float.

—Yes, but what's the use—

CAPTAIN: One mustn't despair with crows.
A nest is a home
for time
away from sand.
A course is drawn
with stick—
a branch leads to route.
MATE: I can give an artery for strait.
To reach the heart, we miss the vain.
CAPTAIN: Circulate the sphere to prove a pump.
It's always there, too obvious for mass—
appeal the case
to enclose an organ.
Pipe out wind to clear a fog.
MATE: How can I believe to blow a wind
that reaches even a child's twig?
When clouds roam, darkness covers.

CAPTAIN: That's the reason for fish
       to dig, to bury
       the light is easy for tide,
       but waters bounce off
       too few can soak.
       Sponge in the foam to cap a head.
MATE: I see now that piles will water up.
       No dams can spike the coming eels.
       To join a course isn't the cause—
       where we all flow, there is the effect.

              —The route appears out of reach—

CAPTAIN: A tide pools our thought
       out of land—roars a swirl
       where energy rays
       a spectrum is given.
       To all our sons, who see colors
       on white—
       we wait for you.
MATE: At times I can really rain to arch
       but the bow sometimes spans a knot.
CAPTAIN: There is a challenge
       so easy to see—a double
       or slip, scouts the trail.
       Blaze a path for those prepared
       always count on rope to tie an air.
MATE: Yes, I can granny a song to knee.
       But melodies turn to quotes

    with a signal—
    vision is applied
    for voice to crack a call.
CAPTAIN: Sail the song of liners to shore's time.
    It maybe pails to inflate the white
    to a point—
    others connect with stars.
    But our horizon disappears
    when mist rises
    the fall
    from waters too sure,
    stay open and channel whatever ferries be.

SCENE II *[Loosened by the Tale, Words Shake the Grasp]*

CAPTAIN: There's a calm that changes bring.
    Between a high or low an ebb
    pulls thought
    to a tension placid with coral and shark,
    where minds return—
    to a source we find
    a tributary marks
    the now of imagined streams.
MATE: I hear your feel
    but remain in move.
    To tend to such a vision, seems to tie
    an albatross—
    rings my deck and ships aboard.

CAPTAIN: Of course, there are whirls that pool.
    All your thoughts are a pirate's word.
    Flag your black with a white bone
    and cross—
    rise a seal
    affix a sphere to shape.
    A stamp labels
    the envelope that foams—
    a fog hides peas
    where the main line cries.
MATE: Yes I feel a sense worth to gravity.
    A land shifts but remains in tow.
    I forget the focus when a mist blows.
CAPTAIN: It's expected to create a loss in sand.
    When crystal clouds
    a storm is stoned.
    To rock a position is a goal for earth.
    Who quakes a trembler will shake your fault.

        —The land is of our making—

CAPTAIN: There's such a reef that catches sprout—
    that grows with red where white was.
    To sustain a pure flower
    buds the coming may.
    But stings impede a process going to light.
MATE: I think maybe the strait sometimes curves
    to allow a diver to see beyond bends.
CAPTAIN: It isn't so deep to fish in a well.

While dreams take a line to surface
a fin, jaws—
clamp and steal
a possibility to rise
in the foam—
it's not too hard to spray.

MATE: Then it isn't the case that a weed can spring.
To a new gulf
thoughts collect mist
to order lines—
tangle pulls straight.

CAPTAIN: It has been sailed to a false calm by horn,
but the mass rises to greet a bow.
Stern courses replace breaks
and bluffs remain by the stars
to eclipse a doubt.

—The horizon is seen to be, but only an illusion—

CAPTAIN: The day's mast remains taut.
Through flow of course
constant changes blow.
An apse to arch
gaps a time with bellows
and twine
while maiden's curl and collapse
a sphere, a fellow navigates,
the circumstance to line.

MATE: Red at night, I learn of colored waves.

Who rises to greet a dawn remains anchored.
I feel to float takes lead
to cement a certain—
fails to depth
and charges night.

CAPTAIN: It's not weed to grasp a pull
but a hull stays hocked to a pawn's move.
If algae greens a growth to stall a sail
what will become of steal remains to forge.

MATE: I bang the pipes but faint lands are seen.
To days in the air
a hope curls a myth.

CAPTAIN: A birth brings grace to a rope's hold.
It's not a neck to know a science.
At times a tide turns to swirl our pool,
while dusted grains spoil a tree.
To route a voyage
stays on green
where blue was seen.

—Letting go a grasp lends buoyance a float—

CAPTAIN: This tale sails to lands beyond the foam.
For shore there is a reach within a bow's grasp,
but the lime shines blue
with a seal's knowledge—
fish as they might
the line catches on air.

MATE: Then one may sink in early June

before ring bears to lick
a salt before
seasoning calls.

CAPTAIN: No, every ship in places pushes a weight
equal to a float—
water holds a wash.
To cleanse barnacles from a hold's grasp
becomes a necessity
to see the sheets inflate to meet
a coming wind leave
to current thoughts
swell with empty branches, bare.

MATE: But then one may thrash when a floats gone.
Left to sink
the bottom exposes empty sand—
where the old fruit fails
to grain any seeds.

CAPTAIN: A danger is there as one eats old weed.
Before a swim the breast must bare
to mind, empty
the whole before
the weight leads
down old fish
by the measure of scales.

SCENE III *[When Shown Free Air, Fear Encourages Fight*
with Old Words]

CAPTAIN: The horizon levels a setting sun to fish,
    waters anoint the glow to cool a doubt.
    Harp and spoon play notes for a new scale.
    Size becomes measured by a single king.
    Fork as bends branch many to a line.
MATE: Sounds as these bubble
    release a gas to air—
    where breath is taken
    seems too deep for bends—
    but maiden's open slowly
    and mind a thought of words
    promise inserts an empty to fill.
CAPTAIN: Don't be slow to dunk once whet.
    An emersion is but feathers to float.
    An old pond dries any hope to water.
    Your desert caps a feel
    once had in youth, forgotten
    as clouds surround a stir to sand.
MATE: Murky hopes can't replace a maiden's touch—
    for some rather swim a line than dream alone.
CAPTAIN: The night is for more than two with foam.
    There remains a truth which illusion is to come.
    Recover your barings to sail the straight.
    Head for home shoulders
    a reception waits.

—But it's written—

CAPTAIN: Some think that fish divide the water
    to opposite shores
    a wave climbs a beach.
    On all sides there is salt to a single taste.
MATE: It can't be that home lands a dock dry
    while we nurse a fish to level the sky.
    Away from sight a vision opens a new.
CAPTAIN: This all only seems coral to a deposited view.
    A conglomerate holds a loose field in two.
    Where waves hide only a fish is seen clear.
    But not to hook a rusty remains a golden key.
MATE: I anchor without a wait.
    Patience bears to hold out a line
    with words in tow—
    it's obviously schooled
    to be written in logs.
CAPTAIN: Tear your pages.
    A captain catches old weed.
    Clean the anchor to hoist only clean breezes.
    The bridge gaps no divide on board's deck.
    To attempt to remain on top sinks a float
    as foam enfolds the mist in any eye.
    A tear drop's the sea to shine in dew—
    any small effort reflects a glaze to light.

—It seems so real—

CAPTAIN: Wield in the waves.
    A land in flight
    seems steady to eyes used to reef.
    But this coral caps an ice
    to float above the horizon
    a mass stretches hopes.
MATE: It's clear to fog that soup stays green.
    Even in a spectrum peas return in pairs.
    For every one, there must be two
    shores to sail from
    a reach distances
    in tow.
CAPTAIN: A mirage mirrors wet thoughts of sail.
    Over blue reflects now
    as anchored dock—
    a journey skips on mind
    to a new shore—
    a promised illusion
    set by foam
    greets bows as a mast
    appears returns one to land.
MATE: In days of fog a circled seems proved.
    To unite two ends
    a knot remains a goal.
    When over an obstacle detects a course to cause
    an effect returns after with riches of rule.
CAPTAIN: It's only a play that fish school together.
    Before curtain an act sets a program.
    To read the lines leaves one under water—

as fall turns colors to strangle a breath.
Rise to gasp a boat
set sail for one.
Divided by lines an actor speaks in scenes.
To cross the ocean casts one a false part.

—It has always kept us full—

CAPTAIN: It's in the waters that night reaches knee.
To fly a white marks caps with line.
Errors of time set squid in clouds.
Typed for categories—filed to ink any real,
red with metallic
rust tainted to drop,
a cold sheet covered thought
remains in cave's hold
waiting for light
a fisherman casts a shadow.
MATE: Well, nets dragged, have sent centuries in tow.
To reach down the ages
the brothers are set in line.
Each remembers a full hold and table set
with buckets on rope
a cup stays heavy.
CAPTAIN: Soon the weight will bend a joint.
Stiff elbowed with an angle
the mouth in degrees starves.
A comfort setting can regulate only old feed
back to depth

where a fire cracks an age.

MATE: We can screen a smoke to preserve a salt
for blows we breeze to dry and take stock.

CAPTAIN: A supply keeps one ready.
For a blast of dried seas
little remains to fish,
an air out clouds a stir
hunted for first flight
of mind a movement recalls.
An old sight with tables before and chained
linked to light, an empty plate
fills a shadow with fin
to break the surface,
a warning gives sail.

—Displaced captains learn richer words—

CAPTAIN: It's a wave to see an old dance shine.
Taken for ground, complete stones sing
of ice watered to slow a motion
with push as words—
act to sign any squid free.
A tangle arms its knots
to grab for wine.

MATE: This once drunk sets feet in air—
to lose a hold a cargo spills its captain.

CAPTAIN: A mutiny does not effect the code.
Set in chrome a wheel defines the course.
Some changes imply a difference to few

but by a crow a cast stays on deck.
MATE: Then sail might circle around to mop.
A clean soap can't swab a loose board.
CAPTAIN: Trips such as gills slice a throat to lung.
Out in air, mist sees cold in frost.
Blown by turns a motion makes some sick.
To lie below a coming deck calls
for each to cast
away with seal—
to pirate a rich cove
buried within a reach
the grasp is left to find.

ACT II

[Prologue: Once convinced of new seas...going
beyond old foam...just space
to reach a new sky...the course
charted in air...only new ears hear the words.]

SCENE I *[Without Kicking, Buoyancy is Freed]*

CAPTAIN: At a height a depth flows free.
　　Unchained by rule any map charts swim.
　　The stroke rises a breast within a beat
　　to heart a matter clings by pump.
　　Pushed into line the main channel floats.
MATE: I've soared to crow enough of new cloud.
　　Where drops pearl
　　a white to rain for round.
　　But edges get shined without a buff.
　　To rub the polish puts elbow in tow.
CAPTAIN: No amount of hoist is needed to anchor.
　　A lift rides a catch with clinging weeds.
　　Loosen the spool and twine will gasp.
　　Freed of hold weight lightens a load.
MATE: To barge in straight a channel narrows.
　　For old dredge defines the course's root.
　　To clear the stumps a wheel misses scale.
CAPTAIN: The locks fail to rise a level of sand.
　　To allow grain finds soil

with rocks sediments form banks
for deposited view.
Old conglomerates mass a hold on waves
to curl free, plants a worm in lime
while shoots spree to a giving air.

—To direct the course words will trap—

CAPTAIN: To take a turn on a wave spin free.
    Twist the line to a right with weed.
    Choking a cough catches foam in air
    where a hot rises to steam a coming vapor.
    In fog a step twirls, leaps and lands free.
MATE: Loose seems to be a tangle without plan.
    A course directs shine and blink in time.
    To make a home roots give a log.
CAPTAIN: It's a trap to crave fish on land.
    Written tuna play songs to sail knots.
    Roped by line an oar times motion—
    to a still the calm claims no bearing.
MATE: A direction shapes the matter to form.
    Weight remains a volume in bounds.
CAPTAIN: Any addition will show too many exist.
    To assure the purpose a shark divides cover.
    Between a lid and bottom, sands the shell—
    an enclosure to define a leading wave.
    Where a mere jester signals in court
    a laugh to judge the page
    the hop bells a gulf.

—Once spoken there's too many—

CAPTAIN: In times of salt a season seems bland.
    To trust the buds a green taste flowers.
    In air an aroma of dense packs all pull.
    To see the change light opens to dark.
MATE: It's without eyes that one knows—
    a sense of fear, a twig loses the root to stick.
    Strong in a coming gale
    leaves to branch a cling
    in different directions
    a course blinds cause.
CAPTAIN: Any bat will feel an affect
    to change from joy, flowers fish
    the strand in pool
    of depth a bearing bends
    a false straight.
    One never sees two without leaving the spring.
MATE: A cool brook soothes the mind in babel.
    Where these bubbles run a fall never stops.
CAPTAIN: To dam the thought lifts the curse.
    In running over falls
    a fig blooms in place of apples.
    A moving sky beckons a command
    to dispel illusion holds a mirror to snake.

—More fish are caught without a line—

CAPTAIN: A joy hides under waves and swirl.

The field shines by moon with pull.
On fluid liquid, lines catch no weed—
stirred by tangle, a trap opens to line.

MATE: To noise it's easy
to see the deaf without motion.
A roar means knot
if hold is full
a mind eases thanks.

CAPTAIN: A full plate retains only scraps to fish.
A catch is complete when a break—
fins to circle a smooth surface as
waves a warning.

MATE: The flag signals ship to avoid or run.
Ever to waver
a mast plants firm.
Seeds on ground
bloom a coming land.

CAPTAIN: To reach a safe cracks in locks.
Never to rise a tumbler can't be.
For when turned a harvest finds soil.
Loosened or weeded the mind sows sand.
Grained a fine milling
blooms below a hold
of pirates on high
sails the altered, sees.

SCENE II *[The Sea is Viewed with Constructed Eyes]*

CAPTAIN: Between the sand and the foam mind swims.
  To make current, tails talk.
  To invent motions, rise to dry
  on salt exposed
  with fin to tongues
  a hot catch worms the line.
MATE: To say ends, remain false.
  To deep, heightens an opposition
  to call sky—
  where flying, fishes
  an imagined bird.
  I see no gulls to graph a point.
CAPTAIN: It's only hollow to assume no bones.
  For up can reverse
  or rinse a sink—
  pipes were laid only to smoke a ring.
MATE: A circle can't be seen from nest.
  A woven home lies
  only straight to meet
  where the opposite is from
  a going shows.
CAPTAIN: In tents a mirror makes illusion to shape.
  A mind runs forms
  to reflect empty fish.
  The head sees sand and infers foam
  to wave where the curl bends
  unfolding lies in tow.

—Breath melts frozen words—

CAPTAIN: To shape a vessel water takes form.
    With frozen space, time empties lines.
    Holding on dock where connections fish
    to catch or drag
    a net defines work.
MATE: When contained, the effort shows ice.
    To cool a cube
    the blocks remain removed.
CAPTAIN: A cut picks the party to stall a choice.
    Where rocks seem glass an incision wakes.
    In turns the dry calls stir
    to rise a float
    tops a level and caps a wave.
MATE: To buy standards a parade trades
    balloons for lead
    weighs a scale
    to allow imperfection.
CAPTAIN: The crystal can cut to serve a tray.
    Dips cracker a cheese for up turned miles.
    A road leads to sea if the shore's desired.
    The coast is expensive when set in rays
    where gold lights a path to deny tides.
    Between pulls, a fish swirls to find space
    where tensions wet, a mind stays fresh.
    By floods a relief is sent with breath.

    —What's held by night is mist by light—

CAPTAIN: To sail ahead, knots measure time.
  For speed is foam when weeds tie.
  Together reflections, wake a mirror to mind.
  No dust can cling where a wet waits.
MATE: When splashed the mist can claim a fog.
  To steer with stars, a course seems clear.
  With wheel and bow a land points straight.
CAPTAIN: Maybe a horizon makes sense to haze.
  But verticals walk on two
  or buy a past
  when nothing is full
  no moon can shine.
MATE: Where is one to grow a beard for pipe?
  To clean a stack a smoke rises sky.
  With dirty passages, can gulls drop lines?
CAPTAIN: Any tern can twist in flight from falls.
  To miss one hair
  the number remembers curl.
  Where attachment means to hold on air—
  no grasp is tight to allow for breath.
  Enough when inhaled a mist clears or covers.
  A mind to sea
  The breezes know the wind stays fresh.

      —Structures held in mind have no room—

CAPTAIN: To clam a shell remains a home.
  With space an empty defines the living.
  Room for mind clamps no thought.

For a pearl's gem a shine reflects.
MATE: How can a meal be made without rock?
     To break the line
     a hammer needs nails.
CAPTAIN: It's not by force that a strong holds.
     But to transverse the current, a swim floats.
     A buoyancy carries a weed to youth—
     where child's weak
     tests a short day.
MATE: Without effort a ship loses the course.
     To stay with stars a dreamer flails.
CAPTAIN: It's wrong to see no shine in night.
     Where the glimmer hides in day's thought
     a knowledge knows only a fish's mouth.
     To hook any polar
     lines tangle a mind.
     For one to catch
     a falling waits.
     To sand a sink
     drains stale worms.
     Where crawls on soil
     reveals no wholes.
     For rabbits without ears
     no magic remains.

          —Notes released scale the dance—

CAPTAIN: Waves glide on foam to wake a dance.
     From sleep, a waltz dreams with steps.

To climb in mind
a beat flows current in any direction
a fish plays scales.
MATE: To glide with time
nothing reaches shore.
But a lost captain claims a course.
Where only a few can see
no river waits.
CAPTAIN: It's an illusion to think of old salts.
Who steers with water
knows the rocks.
From side to side
the motion guides season—
for from stones
a mountain sees a wash.
MATE: Where cleaned a soil
a sail unfolds white.
To lead a purpose
the course stays fresh.
CAPTAIN: No pure clouds a coming with rain.
In sheets the drops dance off sails.
Set for home there's no land to reach.
Where the channel defines straight a bow bends.
An arrow flies in air to part only mind.
For a split in time
a melody makes a scale.

ACT III

[Prologue: What is given remains a knot
tied to words...no speech can free
a mind...must learn to swim...
alone the waters splash...to shores
a course is traveled...a few stars shine.]

SCENE I *[Emptying the Hold Reveals the Sea]*

CAPTAIN: The channels are pure from a deep.
    Gulfs flood a mind without a sand.
    Barred in holds a cargo stays firm.
    To lose the baggage
    remains the case.
MATE: Any container needs to be filled.
    Full with motions
    a ship rocks.
    To wave a gesture
    of greeting
    parts in company.
CAPTAIN: It's not a gain to pick up weight.
    For scales shed light to pass time.
    When ship mates with dock
    to glide a water
    foam bears the measure
    assuring the next.
    In line a point seems stagnate

   for reflection but mirrors
   need looking to see,
   a glass.
MATE: But breakage is danger with a sharp.
   To pack the pieces is the only safe block.
CAPTAIN: When contained in hold a tumbler spins.
   With a steel no door passes light.
   To illuminate a channel
   frees a foam
   in combination of mist
   a being swims.

     —Those on deck dance to a wave's rhythm—

CAPTAIN: A mind empties a hold on waves.
   To toss over, a board floats on salt.
   Bitter dances step in tow
   to a side where common—
   rhythms call the wake.
MATE: To rise the morning gleams off sand.
   When brushed, a shoulder holds a tooth.
CAPTAIN: For an eye, revenge fishes a loss.
   Where nets have holes to grasp a haul
   forget the dragging
   to sand a mirror waits.
MATE: But reflection schools
   a family in time
   of honor—
   the sun brings

back the shine.

CAPTAIN: To polish is away for old boots.
    No heel can cross a line without tangle.
    The sole stays leather when not tanned.
    In light is to return with sun for home.
    Any place can be made to reflect the shine.
    All actions mirror
    the rhythm set by waves—
    to float with crests
    no ebbs will decline.

    —The map implores only a parting knowledge—

CAPTAIN: To reach inland, a gulf forms a divide.
    When separated no company remains in parts.
    Knowledge sands the rough to shine in grain.
    Thoughts confirm a growth
    to strive with water where flows chart
    a map of coming springs.

MATE: The old parchment yellows as sun dries.
    To evaporate the lines
    a thirst stays wet.
    Calling relief a home
    only surface is seen.

CAPTAIN: It's up to the nest to feather a land.
    Shores were drawn but ignored by fish.
    Where a reef waits, old weeds will warn.

MATE: A danger of dock is to slide by a seal.
    When attached to the body

a stamp defines mail.

CAPTAIN: To trust a delivery one must be stable.

Calm the hay, and a bed is found.

Shining by moon

stars fish a night.

Drop the hooks to float by an anchor.

—Without fear mirrors reflect cracking glass—

CAPTAIN: To fear sand, a shark tips a scale.

For motion breathes in glass fog.

Cleared of solid, a sleeper

connects rain with dots—

time seems held in seas.

Waiting for stringing

a poor fisher ties

lines in moon

stars for radiance.

MATE: The illumination is answered by only whats.

To question the deep

foam yields a barrier.

Where gulls circle

a dive needs air.

CAPTAIN: Any bubbles surface a process on foam.

Blown by turns, a spin shapes a head.

On straits a nest hides its roots.

Buried within a tree, family resembles waves.

MATE: The fog is less when tides reveal shore.

For coasts

easy motion with time
recalls a plot
where it points
out of lineage.

CAPTAIN: Only with digging is continuity raised.
Up on last a reflection shows
the past—
illusions to scenes
in lines, regret missing.
Forward connections to join all that's empty
fills a mind
with mirror to shatter a glass.

—The lifted spoon offers a new mouth—

CAPTAIN: As you see or might it's time to wave.
Hold emptiness firm and let water flow.
Of course by design never to be mapped.
Only skidding near surface will fish breathe.

MATE: Please don't leave
to fall in sands
a desert will fill
a hope left
to bargain.

CAPTAIN: No spoons can silver shine to mouth.
The feeding only starts when pangs arise.
To call foam, boils an old weed.
Where bubbles open, the air will clear.

MATE: But to really see there must be a gas.

No fuel is flame when burned out in night.
CAPTAIN: It's up to each to kindle without logs.
A recipe guides, but won't make cooks.
The line pursues an illusion to mind.
When broken, a thought appears on wave.
It's ocean to sum the total of the caps.
With the old, a new watered—
fires burn
a fog.

SOJOURN SO NIGHT

for Jim & Charlie

ACT I

DIRECTIONS: Very dimly lit stage (blues—to a purple mist).
Low, deep, rich bassoon and cello—almost moaning.
A sense of marsh, maybe another planet. Enter Hans
stage left looking around sort of confused—bewildered.
Looking up to the sky between gestures and scanning
the horizon as chorus begins prologue.

PROLOGUE: *Hans your thought was broken…*
Hans the paths crossed many years ago…
View the whole, Hans…One
to a meadow…One to a field.

SCENE I *[A Side to a Self]*

HANS: *[Screamed]* And now I awake to but a field.

CHORUS: *[Softly Chanting]* Pastures bending before sheep.
Pastures bending before sheep.
Pastures bending before sheep.
Pastures bending before sheep.

HANS: The world but a flock, a raving nest.
Incestuous insects lingering thoughts throughout.
Who has heard?

CHORUS: The calls went out, answered everyone,
to rock and stone.
They have written and shoveled
and still sheep graze the roots.

HANS: Is this madness to gather but one lock?

Holding a key turns out a stock. It is by
the light of a moon or a wind set south,
to retrench a closed fist and shout.
The world is too much apart,
standing idly by till the soil is ready—
cannot but a clue uncover earth?

CHORUS: A union, was always worth a joint
for two grown woods, weeds embark.

HANS: *[Shouted]* Enough—I won't plough a single tract.
Too many sheep, the barn is closed.
In wintering I want nothing but water.

CHORUS: Satisfying thirst for green—
Fields—Fields—Fields—sown without,
the lands lay bare to the feud.

HANS: I've fought my turf till wedding bells.
Villaging like a squirrel, I wait for cows.
Pasturing green in but a bluff—
any bassoon brings rain in wheat.
Where soil dries none but a crack is scorched.

CHORUS: It is time to dig the root.
Milk is unnatural while thirst grows.
Give but a lip and sound the horn.

HANS: My life,
a field.

DIRECTIONS: Hans runs stage right and jumps out of sight off
stage. The purple lighting grows more intense and is
mixed with yellow and orange to white. The orchestra
concurrently builds and flares with the light. A loud
shot is heard, the music suddenly decreases and fades,

the light comes down to soft tones, mostly greens. Hans
appears center stage alone as stage becomes misty.
CHORUS: A life in the field defies thought.

Throughout days, separation was made.
You over there cannot be, but are seen still.
Discovering your flock was a distraction in land.
It is to see the pasture that rivers bend.
HANS: I have heard all my life, so it seems

but to a town tailor I'll offer a suit.
If it be in my pipes I'll press the wool—
while those on tracts will hold the land.
CHORUS: *[Chanting]*   The barn is nearly full.

The barn is nearly full.
The barn is nearly full.
It's to you to choose the hills and valleys
between mountain ranges, it is nearly flat.
Where objects are seen, there you be.
Reflect nothing and others will see.

ACT II

DIRECTIONS: Hans walks down a main village street and
enters a tailor's shop.

PROLOGUE: *Never more to not be seen...while vision lasts...*
there will be a first...returning to roots...
a leaf's on course.

SCENE I [The Self Aside]

CHORUS: Now impart to the tailor to mend the seam.
While the air is apparent, shake the dust.

HANS: Good day by the ray, to close a hole I have come.

TAILOR: Welcome aboard and shake the salt.
Feel free to lay out what mendings be.

HANS: Good man, I have two legs at best
but with the help of another, I've learned a truth.
It's not your sowing I need, but please hold your thread.

TAILOR: Son my work awaits by your stride.
While your truth may be worth my learning—
I must flex my wrist to sow my bread.

CHORUS: A fight is to be expected when stitching begins.
Point to the hole and reflect what is still.

HANS: Dear Sir, I wish not to distract your mending,
but to rightly sow you need a firm tract.
Even a surf can hold land before the sea.
It's a crime to wash while still in time.

TAILOR: My watch ticks and yet no work is given me.

I'm kind to a customer but short with riddles.
If no patches you need, I must ask you to leave.
HANS: No riddles are presented in this suite. It's
plain as patches laid flat before you see.
When a tailor can not be, but is still, the world
fits into the eye that thread can not see.
DIRECTIONS: Hans walks out of the shop.

SCENE II *[Despairing Suite]*

DIRECTIONS: Hans alone with the chorus.
CHORUS: Hans you have tried your hand with thread—
but where you place the needle, you may stick.
It takes patience to close the hole—
where one never noticed or thought, a gap
reveals what patches need.
HANS: *[In tears]* What can I do to make this suite?
I've danced all the turns and still remain without a key.
If there is a series to be, I may not have the feet—
to stand and wait for another dance, it may take
a life, to put blood to beat.
CHORUS: Stay and listen for the turn.
Where you may see a lock, you'll discover the key.
HANS: If I have to fish, I'll scrape the scales.
It's the time between measures that I lack.
When the swell begins the water won't hold back.
CHORUS: Listen to the rise and you'll find the room.
It may not be as suite as promised—

but it's up to you to find the dance.

HANS: My feet are as tired as my heart.

To care is to sometimes miss the beat.

Where once I had hope, now I see fields.

CHORUS: The field is from where we came—

to lose sight of green would be to lose the years.

Listen in the pasture and you'll find the home—

where the barn is growing, the sheep are warm.

HANS: I can almost taste this unfinished favor—

where what I thought was sweet is based on bitter.

I can't see the barn until the light appears.

From the sea I'll take my next key and run—

beyond the anchor, I must weigh the lock.

CHORUS: It's not to see where this vision comes.

Allow yourself to walk a course beyond the foam.

Between a tailor and a barber, your hair might grow—

but to jump to sea is a shave too close.

SCENE III *[Another Try Aside]*

DIRECTIONS: Hans back on a main village street. The music

is lighter, almost happy. He enters a barber shop.

PROLOGUE: *Never mind...a mindless mind...returning*

is an advance...from behind...continue

to be...you'll never let locks down.

CHORUS: Hans enough tears have flowed for now.

The tailor requires stitches not from you.

While your thread was good he saw only holes.

Forget what you see is past and ahead to the barber be.

HANS: Hello and high, to trim a lock I be here.

BARBER: Well good to you and sit this stool, it's
with these shears, I do my work.

HANS: Your shears are sharp but won't compare—
with my mind I mow the hair.

BARBER: Son, your speech is fit for a stool with straps.
Keep up your talk and away you'll be.

HANS: Dear sir my coat is not white.
It's with my heart that I see your red.

BARBER: My red is only anger from wasting my breath.
To blow with you exhausts my day.

CHORUS: Hans take the anger for your purpose.
Allow the energy to find its spot.

HANS: Your red is only a color in the spectrum.
From where I sit, I see many others.
For you to allow a single response, is to shave
the head, too close for a trim.

BARBER: What do you mean to critique my skill.
I've lathered for years and still have both ears.

HANS: Yes it's true, you can still wear a hat—
but to hear what I say, you'll need more.
It's sheer folly to shave in the foam—
where you clip too close, there'll be no growth.

BARBER: I have about had enough of these remarks.
Show me your locks and I will trim.

HANS: Sir it is not my lock I wish to show—
but rather that which fastens your chains.

BARBER: I've had it with you, get out of my chair.

I asked about locks and you talk of links.
Those like you aren't worth a mother's effort.
CHORUS: Hans, his mind may seem shut, but not for you.
While he's hot add more fire. Leave his place—
but add a thought to fill his space.
HANS: Dear sir, you've sunk to the base to insult a mother,
but answer who you would be, if denied your root?
DIRECTIONS: Hans stalks out of the shop as we see the
barber's hands drop to his side.

SCENE IV *[Outside]*

DIRECTIONS: Hans at the outskirts of town ascending a gradual
hill that leads to a mountain top from where the whole
town can be seen. As he walks, he talks emotionally.
HANS: *[With clouded eyes]* When to wish but a cry, there longs
not a touch, to record or store or stop.
Yet believing in trees, climbs a far—
gone to wash as in a hope, declining lingers.
By my breath, I take nothing away as it was
and you are a rope of dream to smoke.
I tell of betweens, and fool myself whole.
The world remains out of and was. A complete.
Never mind the hours on a face, I'll climb hills today.
Walk to the horizon, turn up and listen.
There's a still echo near a breeze across.
If we reach, we'll know of rugs and rise
by a sky and below a hope.

DIRECTIONS: Hans stops his climb and sits on a log. The lighting dims and we lose sight of the scenery. Hans is barely visible in rich browns and shadowy gray. Bassoon and cello repeat almost moaning song from Act I. Music subsides and there is silence before the chorus is heard.

CHORUS: *[Softly]* The world turns in but a hope through fields.

To climb or fly trusts vision to rust.

As you find, so you will choose and be home.

To try to see bread in wood, puts hills in place.

HANS: *[In tears]* But I want to walk,

but don't know the steps—

so I placed a wish, in another's want.

CHORUS: Your mistake is your mis-step.

To stride along, projects you out of place.

HANS: *[Becoming more emotional and faster]*

But here I know empty and look for a well.

Alone I seem unable to fill.

I scream at out and bounce walls between wood.

My world is defined as this before.

That occurs, and then—

as if lines straighten the edge any.

We find ourselves beside and long.

A dimension of sea and yet locked.

So I run inside, to be forced out, and show

our humanity is binding snow to snakes.

My case points direction in air—

to agree beyond a nod, and we do.

I cry along, and push the hands between the tower—

closer to chimes and further from home.
I have none but to offer what there is.
Asking sheep where the haze grows,
it may take the earth,
to reach root in but a simple stack—
none awaits.

CHORUS: As you are, you will be.
Not seeing your root, you take water to sea.
Where fires must start, you need to burn.
Another's thought ceases—
and you will no longer be.

HANS: *[Incensed]* Why when I look—
I see nothing but me?
Burning to reflect, I can only mirror hope.
Where what sees is what was seen,
before the break, the field was clear—
now with mud I plow a single tract.
Trudging through the mirth with only boughs,
I bend at the waste and pick a route
that leads to what follows, and returns before
a home can start—
but I must leave.

CHORUS: *[Shouting as if wanting to hit him]*
Hans your home is wholly in your step.

DIRECTIONS: Hans drops to the ground.

SCENE V *[Turning to a Self]*

DIRECTIONS: At twilight, Hans alone in a field.
PROLOGUE: *To reason…ice cries in a frost…between*
breath and smoke…only locks…what
is behind the look…reflects back…
as if to stay too close…closes in.
HANS: *[To himself bemused]*
Now how am I to find what loses me.
Alone I am trenched, dug beneath a star's ladder.
I climb and look up to no one and yet am held.
By a new born tide, I wash what breezes be—
and allow what was faith to fall or fly to find
hope behind or hid as it slid too quickly to past.
And I look up, and world slows, and I nearly stop.
Only to be reminded of the find lost in mist.
There to the fields, I appeal to no reason—
yet revealed in veils of hills, between mountain skies
and loose alibis, still alert in need to hold—
just one moment before flight.
        [Pause]
I wish to want nothing but what was before this.
So I pass on what binds the snow to men.
Not to alter, but to knees bent before our beliefs.
        [Pause]
So much of what turns, is locked in doors—
never seeing light, or beyond the hinge of questions,
burning roots, to clear a path to field.
All hope must finally answer to our need to know.

[Pause]

How is it that what seems to follow, never comes—
to pass, a lock between a blade, and stall in hay.
I have only regretted, the regrets in time, to make
a single choice, and yet the world waits on pins—
placed so precariously, that sheep sleep a day in dusk.
I seem to be forced to face, not history, but a fence—
encircling a geography, mapped by what was about to
    break.

[Pause]

Am I so slow to reason by death that plots
entrench not a wish or want to remain frozen, inert?

[Pause]

Come now to laugh subtle greens, where worms
blue to the sky, light a path around rocks and stumps—
half buried in the belief of flight, bound to yet endure.

[Pause]

Hear the doors
slowly closing, the barn
nearly too full to permit water to seek its own space
leaves.

[Pause]

Such freedom abounds by leaps, once left looking—
behind what was to come, before a harvest halts
the gathering of time, to oneself, before towers—
and yet watching the passing, as a parade of steps.

[Pause]

Now light yet dims, and my vision clouds the air.
Between breath and stars, I cross many roads.

My hour nears an end, where hands strike sounds—
bellowing across hearts divided by walls and faith.
So am I to know not a single tract, but to plow
beyond the fall till frost covers soil? And the ground
from where I stand breaks me apart?
[Screamed] Answer Me!

CHORUS: What you want to know, you can not find in ground.
The soil awaits water, not to see where you've been.
Your vision extends through stars and yet—
you seek what steps can not count.
This is the last you will hear from here to home.
The field is where you belong and where you've sowed.
To others, address and recall what appears as hid.
Show the reason they scream the why into the night
can be light to the day, when it is chosen to see.
No secrets are there to be revealed near loss.
It is only you to reflect and shine a path to field—
where mis-steps block a coming to one.
You'll remove two with a knife to the heart—
not by your blood, but the blood of another—
where no one looks and no separation is seen.
Hans you are on your own to see what others cannot.
To the field you will fail or fly before you can answer why.
This task is simple, but commands a mind—
to dig through soil to discover earth—
as but a place to pass, and embrace in union—
where you are now, and others may finally see.

ACT III

PROLOGUE: *When a voice deserts another...hearts may stall...*
    but before tides wash...a beach is but sand.

SCENE I *[A Self Nearly Touched]*

HANS: To be alone and not to know, yet half—
    I seem to be losing what mind I found.
    When I look to the stars, I see no light—
    and this darkness breaks to no water, I
    need to find what I can't ever know.
DIRECTIONS: In the distance a woman is seen walking towards
Hans. She is about his age. Hans sees her.
HANS: So this sand can hold more prints than mine.
    So what am I to do without a voice?
    Can it be that what called is silent only to stars
    or stares I've focused too intent to climb?
    My hour clocks beats from a far, to swim by waves
    I must never anchor hope from hearts or me.
DIRECTIONS: Woman and Hans meet.
HANS: Let me impose to ring your ears
    just for a moment to pass by time.
    It's not of fear to hold you here,
    but to answer a question that's never asked.
WOMAN: Who are you to stop my feet?
    The light is breaking and I'm nearly late.

HANS: How late you may never know the hour—
    waiting by bay for this ray to bend
    back to a direction that makes no sense.
WOMAN: To talk of sense you clearly have none.
    Yet my feet are grounded sense we crossed.
HANS: Yes, to your heart there is a pull
    that puts sands in the hour about to run.
    Yet before the sun shines, there still is light—
    from where I stand a horizon hides ahead.
WOMAN: Tell me why.
HANS: It may seem why, but it's just a bend—
    to fork through paths past a field.
    If why is where, then to what is how.
    Pardon my pause, but my faith awaits a find—
    still covered by darkness, the dawn is nearly dead.
WOMAN: I see to your heart a burden about to break.
    My mind might run but my feet shall wait.
HANS: There seems to be such a distance before our eyes
    that to hold to a vision clouds what we can't escape,
    but still to stay bended before rays, we hope,
    and yet a head is lost, and nearly the heart stalls, silent.
WOMAN: I feel a loss but my finger can't point why.
HANS: Where is the end we feel a loss to know?
    It seems we are always left just about to.
    And we may break, or worse, and left standing asking.
    What I need to hear has left only echoes of past.
    The dreams now haze of what was clear as children.
    And still pulled, pushed, nearly torn, and in tears,
    How *[Screamed to tears, heavy sobs]*

[through the sobs muffled] can we laugh?
Yet the world won't hear, or maybe I miss.
While the sands stop, I can't count on stars
to reach between flashes while we dance.
WOMAN: You seem to hold so much to past
that you can't reach what flashes now.
HANS: Yes but I fear—
that what flickers only lights an illusion,
which we placed in place of what our hearts hear.
WOMAN: If you listen to your heart you may hear
an embrace that's held without even a touch.
HANS: That sounds too simple to be true.
For the world pains to touch, but is trapped—
between the borders, by what is reached
and what may be touched.
WOMAN: Can it be that by reaching too far
you have only empty hands to show?
HANS: *[Angry]* Woman, it is because my hands are empty
that I reach for something to fill the place
where knowing stops and loving learns
that the head's quest is painful and leads always to death.
WOMAN: Why death? Who dies?
Please answer why.
HANS: The who is you, and extends to us all.
Always demanding why, you are alive, in pain.
In all ways separated from the answer you beg,
while your heart swells and your mind divides
life into questions, pressed together with why.
        [Pause]

As yet the world flies or answers why,
though our hearts crack below strains,
beyond the need for velvet or what's felt beyond the vile.
Thoughts intrude emitting no stranger sounds—
and we listen with pressed ears knocking lobes,
wishing to want none but another, and a place.
So we set in our ways believing goodbys and homes—
and stand between time, testing ice.
And that palace lasts just long enough for spring.
And stars turn and embrace blackness.
And the night forgets the day.
And seasons change imitating spice.
And I leave the world in dreams,
clinging to any ledge that may appear.
But always ready
for cliffs and regrets.

WOMAN: Sir, your speech jumbles my mind
too much to twist or turn my soul—
so if there's nothing more, I must go.

HANS: There is nothing, I fear.

DIRECTIONS: Woman walks off.

SCENE II *[A Self Impossible to Touch]*

DIRECTIONS: Hans at twilight alone on a beach.

PROLOGUE: *To listen to the foam…is sometimes not to see…*
what screams so loud…and yet reaches no sound.

HANS: And so time passes, or seems to slow—

while I wash between the waters and soil.
I can't forget the fields from which I come,
and long to seed what is so obviously barren.
But why should I burden the entire load—
when to speak of homes, leaves me alone.

DIRECTIONS: A fisherman rows ashore near Hans and begins
to unload his day's catch.

HANS: There from the waters is a depth beyond blue.
So easy for you to cast, that the sea becomes a play.

FISHERMAN: *[Noticing Hans for the first time]*
Ay!

HANS: The wind blows from you to me.
And my words reach their source,
never having touched another's ear.

FISHERMAN: Ay!

HANS: How futile to speak of lands between surfs,
when a field is divided, nothing is held.
And to another source we look, and see no reason.
And life is played on a boat on foam—
and the net hauls what the waters drop.

FISHERMAN: Ay!

HANS: So I speak into the wind and face the tide.
Between rising and falling and ploughing and planting
what catches, takes seed, while sorrows will last
their own way, to their own shore.

FISHERMAN: Ay!

DIRECTIONS: Hans walks off.

SCENE III *[A Self That Hopes]*

PROLOGUE: *Symbols lend peace...to what our minds have
        found...*

   to be lacking in belief...by the end of thought.
DIRECTIONS: At noon with a holy man in a holy place.
HANS: Father, you hold some secrets to speak,

   please lend your wind and pipe your cord.
HOLY MAN: Son, my speech is fit only for those who fret

   that to alter, is to amend, what in life lies.
HANS: Please tell me that there is a valley behind the veils

   and that the cloak draws faith from the clock.
HOLY MAN: Son, you are none to me but beyond

   the need for hope, hides the water from our eyes.

   Yet when reached the fountain flows always back,

   and we stop and accept where we still want.

   But no bread is broken, before our hearts rise—

   and with light in our eyes, we close the door

   to the questions that promised peace in the end.
HANS: Father, Father, Please.

   Tell me there is a source behind the scars

   of the burden that's etched on the back of pain,

   where I cried to see and helped others to know—

   that we are behind, one step from what our hearts hold.
HOLY MAN: My son, as you stand you are alone.

   But still wiser from the course you came.

   To pass in mountains, to sea, they are not—

   yet in the end, look again, and see they shade the sun.
HANS: *[Screamed]* NO!

I've fought through all our mis-conceptions.
And struggled with shadows and failing hearts.
And I've climbed from the field and passed the feud.
And broke with the calm we construe as final.
And I've cried as I imparted what we had to unlearn—
to the hearts I met that were hindered by the head.
And now you tell me it's all a tale,
to be told to pacify knees before your alter,
not to be taken beyond where our logic stops,
but to be stranded within sight of our strained symbols—
all for the sake of appeasement and order?

HOLY MAN: Son, you no longer shine back what we mirror.
You have seen with your own light
and yet reflect the dark.
We were all like you and fought the mud
from the soil till we saw the field.
But in the end, we sow only the tattered and the tears.

HANS: *[Resigned]* So I see.
Having reached so far, nothing more is to be grasped.
So you set the standards from a place of knowing
that the altar only bends the faithful's needs to belief.

HOLY MAN: *[Slowly]* It is so.
Half disguised. Half deception.
There is peace, except for the wise.

DIRECTIONS: Hans walks off.

SCENE IV *[A Hopeless Self]*

DIRECTIONS: Hans alone in a field.

PROLOGUE: *When all has been tried...a self is tired...*
   of seeing nothing in the mirror...the heart subsides.

HANS: I am back to the field, but how can it be home?
   To have raced with ears to erase the fear—
   that we are alone and separated, from what we seek
   in an impossible position between soil and water,
   left asking why there is the need
   to look beyond what blinds our eyes.

   [Pause]

   And to our eyes, there are veils clouding the tears
   in the net that is woven between our hearts and head.
   So we fight the strings that pull closer apart—
   and hope we will be able to resolve, before we dissolve.

   [Pause]

   As the fire burns, so to we shall be but ash—
   heaped upon the soil, which stained our hours.

   [Pause]

   Oh, but such a play, the words we used to hope—
   that what is said can be heard before the sheep shall
      graze.
   And the pasture can be pure before the cloak veils
   what cups are hands can form.

   [Pause]

   Almost a laugh, this resignation, bent upon reaching
   beyond the grave to the light-hearted, only empty.

   [Pause]

And the whole is left wanting, never to return
to the place of security that compromises make.
To stand firm, but not frozen in the attempt—
that tempts even the strong to swim
with the current that flows before our eyes.
        [Pause]
And now alone, having first separated the need from
    why—
to see how we live in the shadow of the sun,
glowing intense as the test unfolds,
to our reason we are composed—
as separate notes padded upon the same score,
harmonizing together, in complete discord.
        [Pause]
And that is the question that proceeds why.
To ask in being, becomes life's fact,
to wonder, we are alone—
one step behind what touches the heart.
        [Pause]
And the touching becomes the reach for hope,
to let another in, without altering the act.
We try so hard to hold on to what we lack
that a mist quickly fogs our need to see—
what the mirror reflects, is also in each other's eyes.
        [Pause]
What is left, when I have found
that I reside in a place,
where separation is erased,
but is still to the world in pieces—

out of place,
calling for mending—
answered by war.
      [Pause]
I can't go on.
I have given what is needed to sow.
It is up to each, to mend the tears.
I leave this world in hope,
believing in peace—
calling to the night.

GUARDS OF THE HEART

ALL is quiet
          peace released
After the war
what is it that rages

                    ALL ALONG TOO SLOW
                    known—revealed—shared

              WHERE LOVE

Are we to know
what is lost in giving
what held

            WHAT HELL IS THIS

                              This stopping so near

              WHERE

Strides bound
yet aching to escape
to some half forgotten shore

held as a child in mind
unable to walk of its own accord
caught between the alms of peace
And the arms of war
cradling what hope does lie
in the whispers of the heart

ACT I

DIRECTIONS: A graveyard. Dull lighting—so as to obscure the
time of day—twilight, early dawn on a dreary day. A
body has just been dropped in a common grave—
wrapped in a body bag. Raphael and Sesmosa approach
the grave from stage left. All this while the orchestra has
been playing subdued accompaniment—mostly strings—
no real lead or line.

SCENE I

DIRECTIONS: Sesmosa and Raphael at the grave.

RAPHAEL: Can it be the wrath of God—
    to rock what shakes and confine the files,
    before time finishes the fly with weeds?

SESMOSA: *[Hushed, urgent whisper]* Raphael, not now.
    What lies can we bury?
    What lines shall we cut?

RAPHAEL: Is not our friend before our eyes?
    To close or hide, why conceal?
    If an answer is begged, a line can be coined,
    between us—who knows—there lies the lust.

SESMOSA: We may shine without a cloth—
    or be draped in our own passion,
    for the masses have said,
    what is not moving
    is dead.

RAPHAEL: Yes, but to reach nears never byes,
    the call stalls and waits,
    while what flies, loses what can't be said—
    never yearning to avail, always waiting near water.
    And the world defined by choice and chance
    plays the toss concealing the head.
    While we bury the fear in cloth,
    the temptation grows between earth & grave.
SESMOSA: And we call time to the masses—
    while organs light the darkness to fire.
    And we don robes and sashes and bend,
    what our shoulders won't bear, our knees support.
RAPHAEL: Let us turn to back and reflect—
    the bounces twist time in mind.
    And the hole awaits, what mistakes—
    might take time or lines wrought of flight
    to step in stride or lie, still.
SESMOSA: How is hours to time what might be?
    Waiting action to take root, traces passion
    to hang a poison between rope and cup.
RAPHAEL: As is—must be—balanced in touch.
    Not the holding, but rather wanting—
    the space yet available, encased.
SESMOSA: So as to you but listen—
    the heart harkens, not to lies or lust,
    yet rope tensions what tightens our space.
RAPHAEL: Yes, I recall the names now lost be blood—
    words dripping from the roofs and cleaved in trees.
    Near Autumn, waiting water and changes—

turning days slowly shorter, till the fall.

SESMOSA: And with conviction we sentenced ourselves.
Outlasting the period, out running the bars—
To get to where? A hole now filled
by what remains of the friend we lost.

RAPHAEL: While there is time to despair, hold
what we touch lasts beyond time, embraced.
Ready for chain, we link our starts—
and must combine our pasts, forged without steel.

SESMOSA: So much remains through what is lost.
One perspective opens, and another fills—
the space is never erased, only removed.
Yet calls remain.
And a yes is buried, and the world echoes.
The past comes forward—
and you won't understand.

SCENE II

DIRECTIONS: Mid-morning—just after the shopkeepers have
opened and the children are at school—a small village,
Sesmosa meets an old woman.

SESMOSA: *[Thinking to herself as she sees the old woman in the
distance]*
The years, bring little pain, yet they add.
Everything builds, somewhere, and takes a toll—
not at crossing or borders or bridges, but
rather, the outside coming in and staying—

too close to the beat, but by the river, pumping
echoes to shore washing upon the ears, ringing—
what the mind reflects through eyes before water—
at a time yet called and stalled, somewhere
in the actions yet to take place
yet remembered, somehow.
Though, not yet—
and was already.
As though time stopped, I look
there me, after befores.
And now.
How? I circle or turn or watch or am
involved.
She, there, yes, I remember, not
but feel or rehearse.
All too often, again, yes
there goes I
through time past, colliding forward
never moving
but yet at a place, to watch
and call to companions, to look
and fill spaces—
not with bodies or lies or even plans,
but with the simplest of smiles—
arching a plain back to what connects
before we moved in, before we moved
before we.
And she knows, not on the edge—
but where it gathers.

DIRECTIONS: Sesmosa approaches nearer to old woman.
    She finds her speaking to herself.
SESMOSA: Yes, you must hear or feel too.
    What I think, speaks birds to the night.
    When alone washes air between world and weeds
    yet springing in cracks, placed in planes—
    not in flight, but near borders of thought,
    and what is fought, in attempts
    to feel a touch, placed before minds
    just out of reach, too simple to teach.
DIRECTIONS: Sesmosa stops within hearing
    distance of the old woman
    and listens.

OLD WOMAN: As on white cracks hanging by shadow—
    nearly touching a space, hovering between moon
    and light, as easy defined by weight and blue,
    as to you nears by what can't be placed, but is.
    Somehow too slow to come to rooms to lie to stop.
    Turns yet not rehearsed, or even required, but are—
    taken so lightly and reflected in teeth.
    Where eyes glance at what's not met
    and can't be replaced for never being.
    And I say yes, bounced by walls and straw.
    And we pull at each other in air, and hold—
    revolvings as place as we make.
    And I step back, and you forward, and repeat
    hello to a place, once slipped in an instant,
    shared back to an instant before, and realign—
    the thought now gone to feeling—waiting words

to place lines between distance—
and touch, somehow known, somehow shared.
DIRECTIONS: Old woman doesn't acknowledge the
    presence of Sesmosa. She seems distracted
    and starts to walk away. *[After speech her
    words grow faint and inaudible to audience &
    Sesmosa]* Sesmosa stops her physically and speaks.
SESMOSA: So how does one—
    encounter one, who encounters so.
    Much remains, though much is stalled—
    bogged in mist by what is missed.
    And yet held in mind before what is timed.
    And I wait knowing, too full to fill
    the find of what we lost.
    So I look to no other.
    And choice appears by chance, perhaps—
    or roll, or die, or desire derived not
    by what I make, but what I lack.
OLD WOMAN: So you had to reach to touch, what. *[Pause]*
    My eyes reflect years to your teeth and still
    you pull not by rhythms, not by the moon, not by
        beams—
    but by what seems out of place, wandering in blue.
    Now falling to cracks that you make, that you lack.
SESMOSA: So how does one, share. *[Pause]*
    What we called in air, isn't there—
    a white to fill, what is missed by blue,
    added to the weight that can't be replaced—
    moving forward to an instant before, or to words.

OLD WOMAN: We touch towards what is missed, is shared.
    Consistent as clouds in the air.
    Concealing, what birds—
    we missed in flight.
SESMOSA: No, we have fought till foes are friends
    and graves are full and children sing.
    And what is buried is wrapped in white.
    And the words spoken replace not a thing—
    torn towards, or is there a way to light?
OLD WOMAN: As to speak, spaces become wide—
    not grown in seeds, but placed by hand.
    Where fertile dries the air to futility.
    And a feud fires what desires that lack
    a so simple placement round what troubles the mind.
    So we work to a stall, and mount what horses be—
    and reach false accords on a mare riding wide
    to the spaces found on a loan between clouds.
SESMOSA: Yet we touch what borders on thought.
    Near the edge the masses cry of lines—
    divided by words and acts, apart.
    Taken to holes or graves, the world waits
    to point to causes defined by simple weeds
    springing through woods. And misplaced coffins
    lowered somewhere below roots and vines—
    and we shout at ceilings suspended not
    overhead, but imposed instead, by the walls
    we once deposed.
OLD WOMAN: My dear, you tear at such simple tears—
    flowing through all time, and all the earth,

and all the labor
pushes aside the dirt, to reveal another hole.
Rotting past ripening, waiting what rages—
where to come so close to the cause concludes
a victory, so small, and so apart.

DIRECTIONS: Old Woman walks off.

SESMOSA: And now there's no where to go.
No safe place, no home, no earth or dirt.
Just a hint of a promise, a safe—ravens?
So much craving, from out of caves to wall to ravines—
a flight clipped from a hoped for wing—
and now landed on what ground?

DIRECTIONS: Sesmosa walks off.

SCENE III

DIRECTIONS: Evening in a church lit only by candles, Sesmosa
addressing the memorial mass of person of Scene I.

SESMOSA: So as to push, to what place, why—
when nothing is left, yet nothing undone,
as leaves colored by what drips from sky.
And some know, and some call, and some just
slide—as to slip, between seas—and vision stalls
only as far as to where the eyes are shut.
And we long to hold to the waves about to break—
before the moon, or sun, shades the hope—held
from the center of calm, bruised, too easily tossed
about the foam, flowing from the red left in graves

rotting the answers, so long fought, till earth is tilled
and the toil reveals, another acre, laid plain—
to the clouds, obscuring the pain needed to fall
to the knees, of those bent on rays, altering—
to the feud, between what is planted & what must grow.

———————————

Leaves, sound slips—
such a simple glimpse, as upon glass.
Sliding passed horizons—
hung on the balance of moon.
Stars flow so easily to past, and almost wet.
As to plunge, recalls the moment—
pierced from the worst of men.
And now gone, hiding what was always.
And we wedge years to tears—
as the world works through, not a thing.
Branched by believing in wine and skin—
held so close to the rest, that a start stalls—
by the end imagined & frozen for fear of finding
the one defined by rocks.

———————————

And now, we gather on the edge
overlooking what is plain,
spread before us in red,
as we hold the world to
    ourselves—
and shout out such simple warnings heard only by sky.
And from this place, we trace what tracts are forged—
through our hearts, by the deafness of those to whom

we cry.

And there can be no more waiting
from you on the streets.
While stars shine, we must grasp at the light they cover.
Too easily we have crawled to caves
and bend before the fire—
that we've started, with only sticks & stones, and now—
and now, we fear for our bones,
branching through the belief—
that we planted & watered & tendered,
and the vine chokes.

What is it that we believe?
How can we allow our minds to create such caverns?
Such a ditch, that we throw our lives to.
Such lies that we stand under.
And to shout at the stars makes no sense.
When what light we see, is reflected.
To get to the source, we need not look far.
While what is hid, is covered only by our eyes—
afraid to speak, for fear of drowning in the light of sea.
Such a delicacy, such a balance we must push—
the task at hand may not wait.
And now look at us—
sitting in darkness, watching the candles burn slowly—
down, to the wicked of this world.
We must not bend or suffer this persecution.
Our dead have crossed too many miles.

Hoping for the water, we thirst near the fire.
And we arrange stones to shape our alter—
or to cover the remains, of the humanity,
that we leave in holes.

DIRECTIONS: Sesmosa walks off raised platform (altar) from
which she was speaking.

SCENE IV

DIRECTIONS: Sesmosa in the kitchen of her home—very
earthy, knotty pine—black cauldron, her hair is tied up
and she is wearing a red apron while she cooks at
cauldron.

SESMOSA: Such a stew the world is in.
Left redder by the blood that is used to heat
the tensions that confuse what should be together, apart.
And I stand apart knowing the lies, we must learn
to refuse the simple suggestion of battle—
as if that could lead to victory over ourselves—
isolated, broken, needing mending—answered by war.
Such insanity looming from the part that forgets the heart.
There are no solutions in mind.
Man you have thought too much.
You reason not to truth, or knowledge or home
but to further apart from the wholeness
you so desperately seek.
And the reasons are plain, spread before what you see.
Your eyes have created such a maddening vision—

where your domain rests on the broken souls
crushed underfoot as you stride to get ahead.
And now you are on the verge of losing
the one you had—
not mounted on the shoulders of the world, but rather
the one you ran from, the one you are,
the one you've lost—trying to conquer the one you seek.
> *[There's a knock on the door, large wooden with*
> *metal crossties. Stage right]*

Always a knock, trying to uncover what secrets—
that the passage of years hides, so close to the ground.
As if the very earth revolved about the lies we speak.
And is taken as gospel by the masses forced to their knees
by the need of reason, to control their scattered lives—
and give direction to what broken belief that too many
have died for. Always a desperate push, to shove the dirt
away from our eyes—to see clearly, just once what
we hope for.
> *[Pause]*

And now, to be elected to a position of answering
   the doors,
that appear shut and deaf to the pounding between the
   years—
ringing the passage of time, coursing through such narrow
corridors, that so many try—and are squeezed out,
by their own belief—turning to doubt,
and left embracing any convenient illusion—
springing to fill the spaces, that we've created, between
what we seek to hold, together—and what we are,

alone—apart.

[A second knock on the door]

Always a knock, trying to unravel what riddles—
that the mind pulls closer apart, so shoutingly quiet.
As if out of range of the years revolving about—
the deafness we profess.
And that becomes the canon of the masses aimed at
    the hearts—
left bleeding in their need to realize what seems as
    possibility
and give wings to the hope that so often lies only in
    graves.
Always that deep burning need to find the half that
    hides—
to hold dearly, just once, what we love for.

[A third knock on the door]

Always the pounding, to design what shapes we live in.
To give so much to what becomes another's cause—
to fight, or not to fight the need to be held,
close to what pulls this strained longing to return
to dreams, completely free of any desire
to know, what was left in pools from which we spring
into light, and last our hours caressing memories
as candles, to illume the blackness we've become.

DIRECTIONS: Sesmosa opens the door to reveal a little girl
    and a shrouded figure.

FIGURE: The blackness, seems as closed files covered
    by the weeds, replacing what hope lies below ground—
    not where we stand, but under another's hand, springing

to light the flames, burning silently dark in the night,
as you call to reflect what lies still in balance
between the world and space left listening to the tension
turning days embraced by chains, linking one to another.

LITTLE GIRL: Me.

FIGURE: Time draws near, to what you hold—dear.
What is replaced, replaces you, not to fear—love.
What is heard is held, near as you flow farther
to get closer—apart from the world, you were a part.

SESMOSA: Please speak, I pray, of the time to corse
to what draws before a corpse lies in the night.
Never speaking of the strings secretly pulling the stars
out of reach of those stranded within a promise—
never spoken, but still as a need left pleading
with a knee bent by the weight of a heart broken,
calling in a voice that too few hear & too many wait,
an answer formed in reason, to speak to belief—
to mend in our minds, what is left as hope in our hearts.

FIGURE: As one to another—there is hope.
Not lying by what appears hid, but available—
to those who look, there's nothing to seek.
So much cunning, cuts vision blind to all but half.
Where the other seems hid, is where you look—too far.

SESMOSA: Such a cliche, as if our ears are made of clay.
Not ready for the fires that truth must burn—
to harden a new receptacle to accept old wine.
I pray, to see beyond graves to stop the lying—
still below weeds, as one passes on—to another.

FIGURE: Time draws you on to another, dear.

Where one leaves, another rakes the coals—
to stir the fire, burning the haze, to brighten
the light of the load which you bear to wait.

SESMOSA: How much longer to hold to nothing—
as a will to last enough—to impart enough—
to have a say filled, before night chokes the stars—
left hanging.

FIGURE: The clock strikes—not before the hour is finished.
Allow faith to fill you full, before you hear—
what the world waits, awaits you to see.

SESMOSA: As ready as the world waits, so shall I.
Not to save a self I call, but rather to those
stranded within sight of the word—they need to hear
to be free of the longing that pulls so many to graves.

FIGURE: Such nobility will test the will—
to last long enough, to speak clear—
to those not yet ready to hear, what you say—love,
will pull a piece, will pull a part, will push further
the heart, from which you speak, to mend what breaks.

SESMOSA: What breaks, I can bear to span
the gaps left, from those gone, to those not yet—
needing what I speak to stop so much bleeding,
as the world wars its way through time—
and waits, as hope declines and love leaves—
blown apart—from the trees—dying as we wait
the branches to cross, from the roots on one
to the arms of another.

    [Pause]
And so with patience, I shall wait—

with breast bared to the arrows of those
who use arms, to sling injustice in the face
of those who believe—
that the world works through trust—to cast
the alms, which holds the heart together.

FIGURE: So be it.

DIRECTIONS: Sesmosa closes the door on Figure & Little Girl
and bows her head as the lights fade.

SCENE V

DIRECTIONS: Sesmosa and Raphael sitting on the steps of the
church of Scene III.

RAPHAEL: Such long strides, to climb to where—
we now sit as saviors of a sovereign, city?
Such a pity, to undergo such sanctions
to purify this sanctuary, that has become
the purgatory—of so many masses.

SESMOSA: The masses look to us—to purge—what
their eyes cannot see, for having looked too far—
beyond the walls of the city, they have put up,
to shut up their fear of flowing—free from ties
that are used to sanctify their reasons & their lies.

RAPHAEL: But why should they fear—when with such
passion we have forged passed the lust used
to cement the bonds created by the desires
of such a simple state—imprisoning its subjects—
through their own design, to satisfy brutality—

issuing forth from the same center that love forgot.

SESMOSA: What love forgets, is never in the mind of some.
To call from the center, requires the calm—
that lives of its own life—after its own death.

RAPHAEL: I don't understand why—
some won't take our hand, to hold
to the truths that some have died for.

SESMOSA: Those truths, that lead to those deaths—
are only ideals, set in mind by our time.
And our circumstance, circumvents our stance, alone.
For together with cause, we die, where we need to be—
alone, to be complete—to live—to join together
again passed those ideals, to see the same vision
from another angle—where together lives—before division.

RAPHAEL: What divides the state, seems to divide the mind.
Where we stand, the whole opens wider to the world
engulfing so many broken beliefs, that we give up—
not only our minds, tired of such strains, struggling
within separate cities of thought, that we break
not through, but rather closer to the wars we fought.

SESMOSA: Those wars are waged by the very desire to speak—
out peace, comes not from without, but from within—
these walls, we so aptly call our city, are torn—
wrenched from our hands, grasping the space left
from the removal of our hearts—as the core becomes base,
and we face, the wretched in our lives.

RAPHAEL: Our hearts wrench thought from our minds—
to reveal a solution that leads to blood, flowing
across our ideals, to such grave circumstance—

as our state conceals the liberty without, that
we push, to reveal the freedom within.

SESMOSA: No, to say without confuses our stance,
as much as to say within. Those walls keep apart
our mind and our heart, and lead to the flowing
of thought away from together—to division—where
we separate our humanity & love, from brutality & war—
and wind up on these steps, not any higher than
we were before.

RAPHAEL: So, I see—to fight and not fight, together.
We wage war without, while we are free within.
And no blood flows—from no battle—yet
the conquest is at hand, having already won
over the division that is the separation of ourselves.
We are free to be whole—and set our sights on the cracks
that divide one's state, from one's state & the world.

SESMOSA: And thus we survive.
Knowing the work that must be done—
we go on to teach, to reach.
The masses wait us to remove the weight,
to further the fate of their faith—
as they wait for a savior to deliver
the word that leads to resolution—
to end the conflict of what we are,
and where we stand.

DIRECTIONS: Curtain closes with them on the steps.

ACT II

DIRECTIONS: On a beach—alone, pre-dawn, very subtle lighting
which grows as a sunrise during scene—shadowy
black to orange-red to full lights—Sesmosa wearing
loose, translucent veils—orchestra imitates light.

SCENE I

DIRECTIONS: Sesmosa walking beach, talking.

SESMOSA: O——————— waves
breaking, on the back, of some sure—
thought—about to run—wild, a while.
While I last this brief curl
of time—turning—to itself, to seek
a simple solace from the hour, running
swiftly passed, its own past, breaking
upon the sand, rubbed from our eyes
to remove sleep, to see beyond this shore,
dreaming its own voyage, without us
as sails, to catch, the wind in our hands
and hold, to the mast—as memory—to recall
the docking, of another half forgotten port
somewhere, in its own sound, sealing the water
out of its way—as we float—to some cape
to escape, the drownings—in our eyes.
    [Pause]
Our eyes, so wide to what light

that falls upon this shore, separating
the waters from our feet, as we walk
one last mile—to the land of our birth—
borne, of such strained bearings, breaking
sweet beads of sweat, lost in battle
between the hours of the sun, and the darkness of the
    moon—
pulling the waters, higher than the sand, we once stood—
looking out to see, where the horizon hides—the land
just out of sight, of our salt clouded eyes—
as we trace, the course of tears, across our arms
held wide open—to the sky—to embrace the end,
    of assault
as we taste the vision, that runs from our eyes.
    [Pause]
These steps, we walk alone on the sand as grains
separate from the beach, we make our own way—
as waves—calling to some castle—gone to the foam
that we were once part of—some home—washed
out to sea, we look, where our vision is met
by the blue—we half remember, half forget.
    [Pause]
And now, to bring light to bear, what vision dares
not to look—passed its own sight, shut in disbelief—
held in balance—between the words, and wars
that everyone fights, to break free of battle—
to rise above the state, where we are trapped—
by the borders—we have drawn ourselves—closer
to the shore, we stand, with destiny in our hands—

cupped to hold, what fate we must escape
to be free, to love one another—
as this new light—illumes the sea.

DIRECTIONS: Curtain closes.

ACT III

DIRECTIONS: In a hospital—Sesmosa visiting dying Old
   Woman from Act I, Scene II.

SCENE I

DIRECTIONS: Sesmosa bent over Old Woman's bed.

OLD WOMAN: *[Softly]* My love, the hands are about to strike.
   The chimes we've listened to are faintly
   fading the hours of our strife, leaving
   only brief moments of belief, to replace
   what our minds hold as understanding, out of place—
   with what truth, we have run from ourselves
   to be tripped, at last, by the image that we cast.

SESMOSA: The world only at times, seems in place—
   when we step aside from ourselves to look
   at the division that we've created to secure
   our space, to be ourselves, free of ties.

OLD WOMAN: Yes, those ties bind, not a body with a heart—
   and the space we live in, engulfs our thoughts.
   To forget why we are, we forget why we love.
   And we then are assured of only an existence—
   projected in a place, where we live with no heart to face.

SESMOSA: And to have no heart, is only not to have looked.
   Passed the veils, that the mind constructs, is the home—
   that we die to see, while we fight only ourselves.

OLD WOMAN: To be here, on this edge, alone—

finally to see only what I think,
as I die, the world falls away—
in pieces, that I've placed
together, in mind—in my hands
the love that's there, when we run no more.

SESMOSA: Don't go. Tell me more.

OLD WOMAN: I'll leave you with a smile.
The one I've used all these years
to veil the pain of seeing—too much,
of loving—too far, passed another's
will to hold, having not gone through
the war raging inside—where they hide.

SESMOSA: The War——the war.
We fight without and lose within.

OLD WOMAN: The battle will always wage.
This is our condition, brought to life—
waiting for death——it's all so clear.
What's to fear is a reflection—brought to mind—
to think through what our vision holds
in the mirror, we set ourselves away—
one step apart—from the love—that frees our heart.

SESMOSA: Not one more step. I can't....

OLD WOMAN: hold——
a hope drawn, within.
Such delicate strands, nearly
stranded out of reach of our belief—
held across this shore, to wash
what memories, yet to be found—
in a wave curling back, time

to the hours, that washed us clean
of the need to be heard, through the foam—
roaring silently into the night—I go
to leave you here, bent by a smile—
I pass what can't be held to you,
to hold fast, to what dreams may last—
long enough, to set you, and the world free.

SESMOSA: The world will be free, as I fight
to impart what wisdom that guards the heart—
as you have shown with the example of your life.
The battles we fight, will mean more
than the victories of the field.

OLD WOMAN: With this knowledge, I will rest.

DIRECTIONS: Lights fade—to dark stage.

SCENE II

DIRECTIONS: Sesmosa and Raphael outside the hospital.

RAPHAEL: Is it over?

SESMOSA: It is over, as far as the tears will flow—
to see what peace is passed, fills the heart—
where not yet to understand—I have to call.

RAPHAEL: To call whom—in what voice?

SESMOSA: What strikes a chord in me, strikes
me an accord—to balance what I am—
with what I seek, and the world & you.

RAPHAEL: What? Me, the world—what!
What of the battles of the friends we've buried?

What of the cause, what movement is this?

SESMOSA: *[Building with rage]*

    Slow—— you must not go—
    so fast to the fight, you forget
    what love did begin to boil the need
    to be free—to live beyond, what you see
    as confinement within such a simple place—
    as your mind defines what you see as loss,
    where to let go—releases the love—to spread
    over the wounds, over the battles, over the wars
    over the fights, over the conflicts, over the scars
    over the graves, over the tears, over the long nights
    over the pain,
    [Screamed] Over.

DIRECTIONS: After the last *over* is screamed—stage darkens
    Sesmosa is just barely seen in shadow—everything
    becomes quiet as she speaks softly.

SESMOSA: Afraid, as to be—

    long held tears.
    Across what hangs, we divide—
    one's loss—leaves—branching
    fear, too close to the ground—by rocks.
    Splitting the night into
    light, illuming what hope does survive—
    our need, too tired to strain—
    ties used to bond, subtle feelings
    dissolving as we speak, the space invades—
    hours, striking upon sound.

DIRECTIONS: To complete darkness—a short pause—and

the last part is heard from space other than
the stage—so as to engulf the space with the sound
of what's said.

What space do we share—what comes so close
to what truth that bares wings of its own—Are you here—

There—Love did nearly find—its own way—home, alone
Washed in a world left shouting after its own sound—the space

      Hear, in here
         The Pull So Warm

              Close

                    Nearly touching
                      itself.

LISTEN
      feel.

Astonish—meant, to be free—saved of the world's lies
laid low in a maze of what the words meant

          You are
          too cool in new stars
          shining what light reflects
          peace.

TO BE, comfortable—amid formidable circumstance
     when relief is but an ovation away
     you choose to slide between what rocks
     did balance the world in your hands.

                    THROWN

     Back—the lash
     of what fate unleashed
     the wills of those to come
     to those not yet
     to those we see
     in the light of those

that shine
To be here
In this dream of you

Where did we touch—what lasts

beyond embrace
I reach towards you or
towards my impression of

stone — wild tossed
a slight region of ice

Slides
Cutting what's done by what's left to do
No child don't go—stay, here

Where we stand
waiting the hours
to reveal what we need

in such simple strains
releasing peace from bonds.

Captured
in the anguish of this rapture
watching what I could not help
die—leave, merge   —   WHERE
                                          DO WE GO

LOVE— HEAR
Why Do You Turn

The Night

has no answer
we must hold
Each other in hope

Blue Corner Drama Series

Editor: Kate Alfs
Publisher: Douglas Messerli